OXFORD
UNIVERSITY PRESS

Great Clarendon Street, Oxford, OX2 6DP, United Kingdom

Oxford University Press is a department of the University of Oxford. It furthers the University's objective of excellence in research, scholarship, and education by publishing worldwide. Oxford is a registered trade mark of Oxford University Press in the UK and in certain other countries

First published 2023

British Library Cataloguing in Publication Data

Data available

ISBN: 978-1-382-04346-5

10 9 8 7 6 5 4 3 2 1

The manufacturing process conforms to the environmental regulations of the country of origin.

Printed in the UK by Bell and Bain Ltd., Glasgow

Acknowledgements

Smart at Art and *Hurray for Art* written by Sheryl Webster.

Author photo courtesy of Robert Sarginson.

Content on pages 10, 41 and 42 written by Suzy Ditchburn.

Artwork by Esther Hernando, Kate McLelland and Oxford University Press.

The publisher and authors would like to thank the following for permission to use photographs and other copyright material:

Back cover: p44(br): yasuspade / Shutterstock. Photos: Background p12, 13, 67: oksanka007 / Shutterstock; p44(tl): Dolfilms / Shutterstock; p44(bl): Poetra.RH / Shutterstock; p44(tr): Alex Segre / Shutterstock; p44(mr): ilze kalve / Shutterstock; p44(br): yasuspade / Shutterstock; p45(tl): Insanet / Shutterstock; p45(tr): Susy Baels / Shutterstock; p45(m), p67(mr): shadow216 / Shutterstock; p45(bl): symona / Shutterstock; p45(br): Mehaniq / Shutterstock; p46(l): Robilad Co / Shutterstock; p46(r): finepic / Shutterstock; p47: quietbits / Shutterstock; p48: Savvapanf Photo / Shutterstock; p49, p67(bl): tichr / Shutterstock; p50(t): Alex Timaios USA Photography / Alamy Stock Photo; p50(b): Igolkinaks / Shutterstock; p51: Vectorfair / Shutterstock; p52(bkg): Washdog / Shutterstock; p52: Irina Levitskaya / Shuterstock; p53: Imgorthand / E+ / Getty Images; p54: Matt Keeble / Alamy Stock Photo; p55(t): Benjamin John / Alamy Stock Photo; p55(b): Associated Press / Alamy Stock Photo; p56(bkg), p67(tr): Andrew Cribb / Alamy Stock Photo; p56: Randy Duchaine / Alamy Stock Photo; p57: SOPA Images / Contributor / Getty Images; p58, 59, 60: Sean Webster; p61(tl), p67(tl): MarbellaStudio / Shutterstock; p61(bl): Syda Productions / Shutterstock; p61(tr): wavebreakmedia / Shutterstock; p61(br), p67(br): Alvaro Hernandez Sanchez / Shutterstock; p62: eyematter / Shutterstock; p63: nikkimeel / Shutterstock; p64: Peakstock / Shutterstock; p65: antoniodiaz / Shutterstock; p66(t): Rawpixel.com / Shutterstock; p66(b): Syda Productions / Shutterstock; p68(tl): SeventyFour / Shutterstock; p68(tr): lunamarina / Shutterstock; p68(b): NDAB Creativity / Shutterstock.

Every effort has been made to contact copyright holders of material reproduced in this book. Any omissions will be rectified in subsequent printings if notice is given to the publisher.

FSC
www.fsc.org
MIX
Paper | Supporting responsible forestry
FSC® C007785

In this book ...

OXFORD
UNIVERSITY PRESS

Have a go!

wh as in wheel

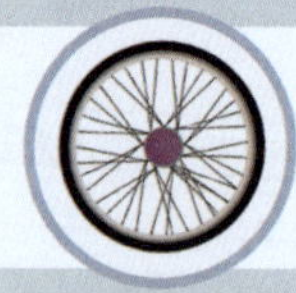

ph as in elephant

ew as in newt

oe as in doe

au as in launch

ey as in key

a-e as in snake 

e-e as in athlete 

i-e as in kite 

o-e as in phone 

u-e as in flute 

c as in circle 

Have a go!

your

ask

should

would

could

asked

house

mouse

water

want

very

Read this book if ...

you like

HELPING PEOPLE

or

HAVING FUN WITH ART!

In this book, Rose puts her artistic talents to good use.

STOP AND THINK

Think of a time when you had fun with art. What made it fun?

SMART AT ART

Written by Sheryl Webster
Illustrated by Esther Hernando

Rose

Mum

Luke, Rose's best mate

Rose's classmates

Rose was glad it
was **HOME TIME**.

"What's the matter?" asked Luke. He always sat next to Rose on the bus.

"I didn't have a very good day,"
Rose sighed.

"I felt like the day flew past!" said Luke.

"You would think that.
You **enjoy** all the lessons!"
Rose said.

"Which lessons do you like?"
asked Luke.

"The **ONE** lesson I like is art," said Rose. She gave Luke her art book.

As soon as Rose stepped into the house, her mum appeared.

We have a new space
for the **Kids' Club**.

Rose played games there with her mates, but it was quite cramped. A **NEW SPACE** would help a lot.

"The club leader has asked me to paint it!" said Mum with a smile.

Will you help me?
YES!

There was just **ONE RULE**.
It had to be complete for
the launch next week.

"This is such a **BIG** space.
We need **LOTS OF PAINT!**"
Rose exclaimed.

Rose planned the painting.
She showed Mum.

They had **lots of fun** painting.

When Rose and Mum finished, they felt **PROUD**.

The next day,
Rose's classmates
were chatting
about the club.

Rose wanted to tell them, but she felt a bit **DAUNTED**.

What if they did not like it?

That evening, all the children rushed to see the new space.

Cute!

"These animals look like yours," Luke grinned. "I love the **BIG** elephant and mini mouse!"

"Did **YOU** do these?" asked Joe, a classmate. Rose nodded ...

The children **CLAPPED** and took pictures on their phones.

Rose and her mates went outside.
"It's quite dull outside," said Joe.

Mickey, the club leader, joined them.

"Yes!" whooped her classmates.

We could
ALL paint it!

So, with **Rose's help**,
that is what they did.

Look back

1 Look back at p30. Do you know what 'daunted' means?

2 How do you think Rose felt at the launch?

This book celebrates lots of different artists.

STOP AND THINK

Have you made art for a display? What did you make?

Hurray for Art!

Written by Sheryl Webster

Contents

Art is everywhere

Art is found inside ...

and outside.

There are **DIFFERENT WAYS** to make art.

Sculptures

Sculptures are made from clay, stone, wood or metal. They may be carved or formed into shape.

People travel a long way to visit these sculptures.

This bright sculpture is part **food** and part **animal**.

What are they?

A: Sheep and banana!

Would **YOU** like this big sculpture in your home?

It would be hard to forget!

POP ART

Artists use common objects to make bright pictures. Look at this food tin art.

Pop art can be letters or a name.

Sometimes it might be of people – like this **shocked** face!

You can make pop art with bright paint.

Street art

This is art we see in public places.

This artist makes art before people are awake.

Stik paints to express his feelings.

He made the **TALLEST** street art in the UK!

Stik

Swoon wanted her art to be seen. She stuck art up in public places!

Swoon

Street artists do not just paint at **ground level**. This artist needed help to reach those top bricks!

Art for smiles!

This artist makes art to make people smile.

His pictures can be found in lots of places!

jumpers

caravan

People have **FUN** getting a picture next to his art.

SMILE!

Jobs in art

Let's take a look at some jobs.

Artists illustrate books, comics and adverts.

Manga artists **draw** pictures to form a **plot** in a book.

In Japan, manga means 'cartoon'.

Art therapists help people who might feel quite sad. Art helps them to express their feelings.

Some people make **displays** of paintings or sculptures.

Some people take interesting **SNAPS**. The pictures might be put into books. They might be displayed for people to see.

You and art

Which art did **YOU** like best?

You could make art for your home!

Make a sculpture.

Draw a **cartoon.**

Paint a picture.

Look it up

displays: objects placed for people to look at

ground level: at the same level as the ground

plot: what happens in a tale

Index

Ha! Ha!

What is green and smells like red paint?

Green paint!